T0052424

Simple Machines
Inclined Planes

by Martha E. H. Rustad

CAPSTONE PRESS
a capstone imprint

Little Pebble is published by Capstone Press,
1710 Roe Crest Drive, North Mankato, Minnesota 56003
www.mycapstone.com

Library of Congress Cataloging-in-Publication Data
Names: Rustad, Martha E. H. (Martha Elizabeth Hillman), 1975– author.
Title: Inclined planes / by Martha E.H. Rustad.
Description: North Mankato, Minnesota : Capstone Press, 2018. | Series:
    Little pebble. Simple machines
Identifiers: LCCN 2017031581 (print) | LCCN 2017035879 (ebook) |
    ISBN 9781543500899 (eBook PDF) | ISBN 9781543500776 (hardcover) |
    ISBN 9781543500837 (paperback)
Subjects: LCSH: Inclined planes—Juvenile literature.
Classification: LCC TJ147 (ebook) | LCC TJ147 .R877 2018 (print) | DDC
    621.8—dc23
LC record available at https://lccn.loc.gov/2017031581

Editorial Credits

Marissa Kirkman, editor; Kyle Grentz (cover) and Charmaine Whitman (interior), designers;
Jo Miller, media researcher; Katy LaVigne, production specialist

Image Credits

Capstone Studio: Karon Dubke, 17, 21; iStockphoto: /kali9, 11, Shinyfamily, 15; Science
Source: Photo Researchers, Inc., 7; Shutterstock: BCFC, 9, Caron Badkin, 13, Grandpa, 22,
Marcel Derweduwen, cover, 1, Sajee Rod, 5, wavebreakmedia, 19

Design Elements

Capstone

Printed in the United States   5878

Table of Contents

Help with Work

Work is hard!

We need help.

Use a simple machine.

These tools help us work.

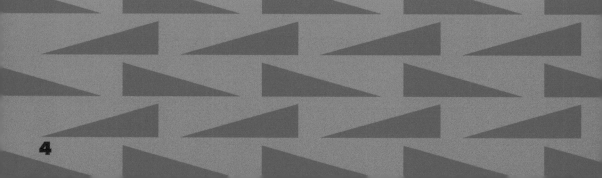

inclined plane

An inclined plane is a ramp.
We move a load up or down
the ramp.

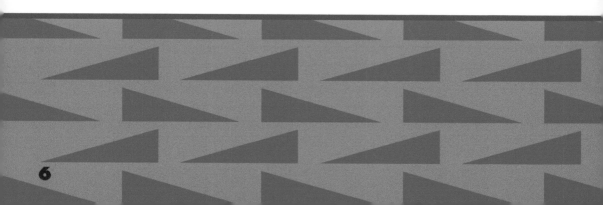

load

ramp

Move a Load

One end is low.

The other end is high.

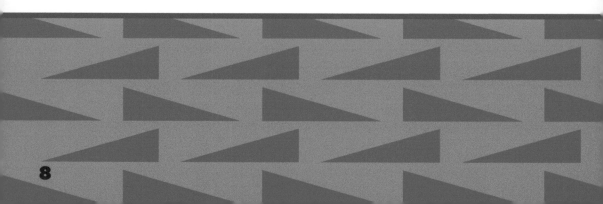

A load sits at the bottom.

We move it up.

load

The load moves to the top.

It takes longer to get there.

But the work is easier.

Everyday Tools

The train is at the bottom.

Push!

The train goes up the ramp.

A slide is an inclined plane.

Whee!

I go down fast.

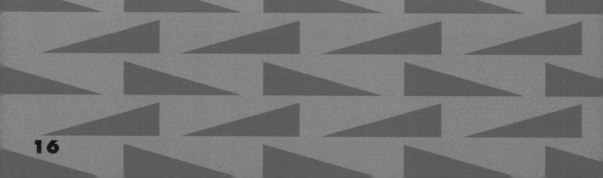

Steps are an inclined plane.

Climb!

We can reach the top.

We use a simple machine.

It makes work easier and fun.

Glossary

inclined plane—a simple machine that makes moving a load up or down easier; it is sloped with one end higher than the other, like a ramp

load—an object that you want to move or lift

simple machine—a tool that makes it easier to do something

tool—an item used to make work easier

work—a job that must be done

Read More

Miller, Tim and Rebecca Sjonger. *Inclined Planes in My Makerspace.* Simple Machines in My Makerspace. New York: Crabtree Publishing, 2017.

Schuh, Mari. *Playing a Game: Inclined Plane vs. Lever.* Simple Machines to the Rescue. Minneapolis: Lerner, 2016.

Weakland, Mark. *Fred Flintstone's Adventures with Inclined Planes: A Rampin' Good Time.* Flintstones Explain Simple Machines. North Mankato, Minn.: Capstone Press, 2016.

Internet Sites

Use FactHound to find Internet sites related to this book.

Visit www.facthound.com

Just type in 9781543500776 and go.

Super-cool stuff!

Check out projects, games and lots more at
www.capstonekids.com

Critical Thinking Questions

1. What do we move up or down a ramp?

2. What is different about the two ends of an inclined plane?

3. What types of inclined planes have you used? How did they help you?

Index